IRISH PROVERBS

First published in 1993 as
The Wasp in the Mug: Unforgettable Irish Proverbs
This edition, containing new material.
published 1999 by
Mercier Press
PO Box 5 5 French Church St Cork
Tel: (021) 275040; Fax: (021) 274969;
e.mail: books@mercier.ie
16 Hume Street Dublin 2
Tel: (01) 661 5299; Fax: (01) 661 8583;
e.mail: books@marino.ie

Trade enquiries to CMD Distribution
55A Spruce Avenue
Stillorgan Industrial Park Blackrock
County Dublin
Tel: (01) 294 2556; Fax: (01) 294 2564
e.mail: cmd@columba.ie

© Gabriel Rosenstock 1993, 1999

ISBN 1 85635 282 X

10 9 8 7 6 5 4 3 2 1

A CIP record for this title is available
from the British Library

Cover design by Penhouse Design
Printed in Ireland by ColourBooks,
Baldoyle Industrial Estate, Dublin 13

Irish Proverbs

in Irish and English

Gabriel Rosenstock

Mercier Press

CONTENTS

A NOTE ON THE TRANSLATIONS

In many cases I have gone for a rhyme in English. This lengthens the phrase, in some instances, with a slight change of colour or emphasis. Here and there I have added a comment or interpretation, not superfluously, I hope. You'll find these at the back. The selection is a personal one: proverbs I have noted, or heard, and enjoyed over a period of twenty years or so.

Gabriel Rosenstock
Baile Átha Cliath

Arrangement of Proverbs

The arrangement might seem haphazard or arbitrary to some readers. I have deliberately chosen to avoid repetitiveness and decided against grouping proverbs under various thematic headings – food, drink, old age etc. Think of this collection as a bag of liquorice allsorts. Dip in, now and again, when you feel the urge. Don't keep them all to yourselves. They're for sharing.

INTRODUCTION

The wit and wisdom of the Gael are tightly packed in the proverb. Irish proverbs elucidate the Irish mind in a distilled fashion, frequently throwing light on aspects of social and cultural history. Certain media mandarins who question the very existence of 'an Irish mind' are themselves, generally, unfamiliar with native lore.

'Ba é chéad bhia ar an sliogán dó na scéalta sin' means 'he was nurtured on those tales'. But look how the Irish language concretises things – a great boon in this age of linguistic obfuscation: literally it says 'the first food on the shell for him was those tales'. The image of the shell (used as a plate) springs to the visual mind immediately.

Traditionally, the Gaelic mind has abhorred abstractions so that abstract truths are represented here by metaphor and simile drawn from the natural world. That natural world is one of endless variety. Thus, in Irish a potato isn't just a potato. Munster people say *práta* (prawtha) and Connacht people say *fata,* giving rise to the observation that the Connacht people would have washed, boiled and eaten their potatoes by the time it took the Munster people to say *práta!*

But what about *falcaire*, an old seed-potato, or a dried-up one, used to describe a deceptive person! *Prochán* is a potato roasted in ashes – or a podgy person. *Sliomach* is a soft potato or a spineless individual, *creachán*, a small potato or a puny person.

The proverbial mind, therefore, creeps into single words, investing them with praise, derision or whatever. One word, *stadhan*, describes a flock of birds over a shoal of fish. One word, *gabhgaire*, describes an onlooker at a game of cards. The word *canúnaí* means someone interested in or addicted to dialect. Where else in the world would you find such an addiction!

I have read nature poetry, proverbs and weather lore to inner-city children who have never seen a frog or a heron or touched bog-cotton or enjoyed the aroma of turf. And yet, teachers and librarians assure me that their minds are fired by wildlife, as if some ancient memory of mountains and the sea still lingers on in the genetic pool. Fanciful? Perhaps.

The mind that created these proverbs no longer exists in its full integrity: the language is thinning out, where it has not actually been stilled, and with this loss comes a less sophisticated response to the diversity of nature and an impoverished nomen-clature. But we can absorb that mind, to a lesser or greater degree. At least a hundred of these proverbs are a living part of my own consciousness, my mental furniture. Their usefulness is not merely by way of repartee. In a way they form the groundwork for a mental Ninja-culture, an adroitness, a sharpness always to hand when the dross and morass of contemporary culture threatens to stifle us, utterly.

Irish is no mere folksy language of quaint expressions. It has the oldest, most sophisticated literature in Western Europe. To this day eighty or so books are published yearly in Irish. Many see the language in a state of inevitable decline. Estimates of the number of native speakers sometimes fall below the 20,000 mark.

It would be a tragedy beyond words if the Irish language disappeared and those of us who know and love the language would not wish to see one single word perish. *Floreat!*

NA TRÍ SÚILE IS GÉIRE:
Súil na circe i ndiaidh an ghráinne,
Súil an ghabha i ndiaidh an tairne,
Agus súil ainnire i ndaidh a grá gil.
The three sharpest eyes:
The hen's eye on the grain,
The blacksmith's eye on the nail,
The loving eyes of a maid.

D'fheannfadh sé dreancaid ar a craiceann.
He'd flay a flea for its skin.[1]

Caora mhór an t-uan i bhfad.
To carry a lamb is no great load
But it's a sheep you'll have a mile down the road.

Cuid an daimh den eadra.
The ox's part in the milking operations.[2]

Cosúlacht báis sop i ndiaidh na circe.
A wisp of straw on a hen's rear:
Death will come in a day and a year.[3]

Ní baol don bhacach an gadaí.
The beggar need not fear the thief.

Sceitheann fíon fírinne.
Truth is spilled
When wine is swilled.

Is goirt iad na deora, na deora a siltear
Ach is goirte go mór iad na deora nach siltear.
Bitter the tears, the tears that are shed,
Bitterer those that remain in the head.

Is mó an torann ná an olann
Mar a dúirt an chaora leis an ngabhar
a bhí á lomadh.
Much cry and little wool,
As the sheep said of the goat being shorn.

Tabhair do phóg do chois an ghiorria.
Kiss the leg of a hare![4]

Ná bí abhus is a bheith thall
Ná bí thall is a bheith abhus –
Nó má bhíonn tú abhus is a bheith thall,
Ní bheidh tú thall ná abhus.
Don't be here when you should be there;
Don't be there when you should be here
Because if you're here and there
You won't be anywhere.[5]

Cnuasach na gráinneoige.
He gathers and he gathers and he hides his store
    away –
But where the hell he put it, the hedgehog cannot
    say.

Gach breac mar a shnámhann ach an scadán ar a
    dhrom.
Every fish as it swims, but the herring on its back.[6]

Sin méadú ort! arsa as dreoilín
Nuair a rinne sé a mhún san fharraige.
There now, you're bigger! – said the wren to the sea
(Having done a pee . . .)

Mar a dúirt an gabhar bacach – ní fheadar
Cé acu is fearr luas nó moilleas.
As the lame goat said: I don't know
Which is the better, to go fast or slow.

Ní féidir fear gan ceann a chrochadh.
You cannot hang a headless man.

Bean ag gol, bean ag gáire,
Bean eile agus a cuid putóg lena sáile,
Cé acu sin an bhean is mó náire?
Is é sin an bhean a bhíos ag gáire.
A woman with tears in her eyes, a woman with a
    laughing face,
A woman with her guts strewn all over the place,
Which of these most disgraces her race?
She with the laughing face![7]

Glór poiche i muga.
The voice of a wasp in a mug.[8]

Imíonn an méanfach ó dhuine go duine
Mar a imíonn an spideog ó bhile go bile.
A yawn can pass from you to me
Like a robin, from tree to tree.

Bainne cíche circe a bhleán
In adhairc mhuice
Agus a mheascadh le cleite cait.
Breastmilk from a hen
Milked into a pig's horn
And stirred with a cat's feather.[9]

Bean mhic is máthair chéile
Mar a bheadh cat is luch in aghaidh a chéile.
The son's wife and the mother-in-law,
Cat and mouse, tooth and claw!

Ní beag a bheith go dona, ach gan a bheith go dona
  faoi.
It's bad enough being miserable without being
  miserable about it.

'Beidh mise i bpáirt leat,'
Mar a dúirt an sionnach leis an gcoileach.
'Let's be partners, old stock!'
Said the fox to the cock.

Síol don phiast agus síol don chág
Síol chun lofa agus síol chun fáis.
A seed for the worm, a seed for the crow,
A seed to rot and a seed to sow.

Lán gabhála de ghainimh trá,
Lán mála den ghaoith aduaidh,
Comhairle a thabhairt do mhnaoi bhoirb
Nó buille ribe ar iarann fuar.
Put sense into a woman's mind?
Try filling a bag with the north wind!
Try carrying an armful of sand from the shore
Or beating cold iron with a little rib of hair.

Is fearr fuíoll fonóide ná fuíoll formaid.
Better by far to be laughed at a lot
Than be envied by all for the little you've got.

Fear óg diagaithe ábhar diabhail seanduine.
A pious young man – he'd move you to tears –
A randy old divil in later years.

Uan dubh ar dtús,
Searrach is a thóin leat,
Cuach i dtaobh na cluaise clí,
Is ní éireoidh an bhliain leat.
A black lamb in front of you,
A foal that turns his rear to you,
A cuckoo in your left ear,
It will be a bad year![10]

Nuair a lasfaidh tú déanfaidh tú tine,
Arsa an sionnach nuair a chac sé ar an sneachta.
You'll light up soon and you'll glow,
Said the fox who shat in the snow.[11]

Cuir síoda ar ghabhar agus is gabhar i gcónaí é.
A goat is a goat, goat born and bred
Though you clothe him in silk from hoof to head.

Ceann cíortha a dhíolas na cosa.
Good grooming, with hair kept neat –
Whatever your faults – will keep you on your feet.

Sháraigh na mná Harry Stottle
Is sháraigh Harry Stottle an diabhal.
Women were too much for Aristotle
And Aristotle was too much for the devil.

Tá cluasa fada ar mhuca beaga.
Little pigs have big ears.[12]

Cuileog an chairn aoiligh is mó a ghníos torann.
The fly on the dung-heap is the noisiest of all.

An rud nach bhfuil is nach mbeidh,
Nead ag an luch i bhféasóg an chait.
Something that never will be – and that, my friend,
    is that –
The nest of a mouse in the whiskers of a cat.

Trí shórt ban nach féidir le fear a dtuiscint:
Bean óg,
Bean mheánaosta,
Seanbhean.
Three types of women a man can't understand:
A young woman,
A middle-aged woman,
An old woman.

'Is deas í an ghlaineacht,' arsa an sraoill,
Is í ag glanadh an phláta le heireaball an chait.
'Cleanliness is a nice thing,' said the slattern,
Cleaning the plate with the cat's tail.

Scil Dhiarmada i gcac na ngabhar,
A d'ith iad in áit airní!
The skill of Diarmuid who, everybody knows,
Ate goat-droppings – thinking they were sloes![13]

Tá a spuir féin agus capall duine eile aige.
He has his own spurs and another man's horse.

Caill do chlú agus faigh arís é,
Agus ní hé an rud céanna é.
Lose your good name,
Regain it – it's never the same again.

Ní sheasann sac folamh.
An empty sack won't stand.[14]

Bean bhreá, nó capall bán, nó tigh ar ardán,
Sin trí mhallacht an chlutharacháin.
A beautiful woman, a white horse, a house on a
    height:
The curse of the leprechaun! What a fright!

Scinneann gráinne ón scilligeadh.
A grain escapes from the shelling.[15]

Na trí glórtha is binne:
Meilt bhró, géimneach bó is béic linbh.
Three sounds that are sweetest:
Quernstone grinding, cow lowing, child screaming.

Na trí rian is giorra a fhanas:
Rian éin ar chraoibh,
Rian bric ar linn,
Rian fir ar mhnaoi.
Three traces soon gone:
On a branch – a bird,
In a pool – a trout,
On a woman – a man.

Ná trí héisc is mire:
rotha,
ranga,
agus rón.
The fastest in the sea:
The ray,
The mackerel,
And the seal.[16]

Súil iolair i gceo,
Súil con i ngleann,
Súil mná óige ar aonach.
The eagle's eye in the mist,
The hound's eye in the glen,
The eyes of a girl on young men.[17]

Na trí beaga is fearr –
Beag na coirceoige,
Beag na gcaorach,
Agus beag na mná.
The best of the littlest –
The little hive,
The little sheep,
The little woman.

An fhaid a bheidh naosc ar móin is gob uirthi.
As long as the snipe on the moor has a beak.[18]

Teachtaire an fhiaigh ón Áirc.
Hark! Hark! The raven-messenger of the Ark[19]

Is mór an náire do Mháire Ní Dhálaigh
A bheith ar deireadh, a bheith ar deireadh.
Mary Daly, have you no shame?
Last again, last again![20]

Bhearrfadh sé luch ina chodladh.
He'd shave a sleeping mouse!

Bean mar mhuic ;
Bean mar chirc;
Bean mar chaora.
Piggish woman;
Hennish woman;
Sheepish woman.[21]

Sceinneann éan as gach ealta.
From the flock in the sky one bird will fly.[22]

Nuair a chacann gé cacann siad go léir.
Let one goose shit and they're all at it.[23]

Spáráil na circe fraoigh ar an bhfraoch.
The moorhen sparing the heather.[24]

Ní haon mhoill ar fhaoileán
Nuair a thagann an scadán.
Herring in sight,
Seagull in full flight.

Is maith an chearc nach mbeireann amuigh.
Good the hen that lays within.[25]

An chearc ar fad is an anraith.
The whole hen and the soup[26]

Ubh na circe duibhe.
The black hen's egg.[27]

Níor thacht an bia riamh máthair na sicíní.
Food never choked a mother of chickens.[28]

Ó bearradh na rónta
Before you were born,
When seals were shorn ... [29]

Dála an mhadarua agus na silíní.
Like the fox and the cherries.[30]

Ló go n-óiche an luch.
The mouse is a fright –
From morning to night![31]

Tá an earc luachra ina bholg.
The newt is in his belly.[32]

Codladh an ghiorria.
The sleep of the hare.[33]

Fear na caorach beirithe.
He boiled his sheep.[34]

Ag cuimilt saille de thóin na muice méithe.
Rubbing fat on the fleshy pig's arse.[35]

Is olc an banbh ascall agat é.
It's a bad piglet you've under your arm.[36]

Aicearra an chait tríd an ngríosaigh.
The cat's shortcut through the embers.[37]

Fuadach an chait ar an domlas.
The cat chasing the uneatable.[38]

*Is é an madarua is túisce a fhaigheann boladh a
bhroma féin.*
The fox is the first to smell his own fart.

Tógfaidh dath dubh ach ní thógfaidh dubh dath.
Colour will take black but black will not take
colour.[39]

*Ní dheachaidh Harry Stottle amach ar oíche
fhómhair.*
Aristotle never went out on an autumn night.[40]

*Báisteach ó Dhia chugainn is gan é bheith fliuch
Is cuid an lae amárach go ndéana sé anocht.*
Rain from God and let it be light
And may tomorrow's share come down tonight.

Lá millte na móna lá fómhair an chabáiste.
Turf ruined, cabbage harvested.[41]

Is í an dias is troime is ísle a chromann a ceann.
The heaviest ear of corn bends lowest.[42]

Bí bog crua ar nós eireaball na bó.
Be soft and hard like the cow's tail.[43]

Téann an bainne sa gheimhreadh
go hadharca na mbó.
In winter the milk goes to the horns of the cow.[44]

Gheobhair in aoileach na Bealtaine é!
It's lost, you say?
You'll find it in the dung of May.

Is sleamhain an lao nach lífidh a mháthair féin í.
Slippery the calf that its own mother won't lick!

Ceathrar sagart gan a bheith santach,
Ceathrar Francach gan a bheith buí,
Ceathrar gréasaí gan a bheith bréagach –
Sin dhá fhear déag nach bhfuil sa tír.
Four priests that are not greedy,
Four Frenchmen that are not tanned,
Four cobblers not deceitful –
A dozen you won't find in the land.

Is fearr seo é ná cá bhfuil sé.
Better 'Here it is!' than 'Where is it?'

Chomh leitheadach leis na cuacha.
As conceited as the cuckoos.

Chomh Gaelach le muca Dhroichead Átha.
As Irish as the pigs of Drogheda.

Chomh dubh le tóin an phúca!
As black as the Pooka's arse![45]

Chomh géar-radharcach le gainéad.
As sharp-sighted as a gannet.[46]

*Chomh díreach is atá an chnámh i ndroim na
    lachan.*
As straight as a bone in the back of a duck.

Chomh dall ar meisce le coinín.
As blind drunk as a rabbit.[47]

Chomh hata le frog san fhómhar.
As swollen as a frog in autumn.

Chomh bocht le bairneach.
As poor as a limpet.

Chomh bréan le pluais an mhadarua.
As smelly as the fox's den.

Chomh caoch le bonn mo bhróige.
As blind as the sole of my shoe.

Chomh casta le hadharc gabhair.
As twisted as a goat's horn.

Fiach nó iascach ní raibh air riamh an rath,
*Ach an té a leanann béal an chéachta ní folamh a
    bheidh a shac!*

Hunting and fishing never bring luck –
Follow the plough and earn an honest buck![48]

Dála reithe Sheáin na Buile!
Like Mad John's ram![49]

*B'fhearr liom a bheith ag fáscadh
gainimhe faoi m'fhiacla.*
I'd rather crunch sand under my teeth.

Faoi mar a chacfadh an t-asal é!
As the donkey would evacuate it![50]

Chomh trom sin go n-íosfá le spúnóg é.
You could eat it with a spoon it's so heavy.[51]

Chomh sleamhain le bolg eascún.
As slippery as an eel's belly.

Chomh tiubh le tiul.
Like a hail of bullets.

Chomh pioctha le sagart.
As neat as a priest.

Chomh ramhar le ministir.
As plump as a vicar.

Chomh sámh le liopadaileap.
As tranquil as a basking shark.

Bás Aoine,
Tórramh Sathairn
Agus sochraid Domhnaigh.
Friday death,
Saturday wake,
Sunday funeral.[52]

Bíonn ceathanna sneachta um Bhealtaine
Agus cailleacha ar leabaidh ag srantarnaigh
Agus mairbh ag tarraingt ar theampallaibh.
Snow falling in May,
Hags snoring in bed all day
And the dead being carted to the grave.

Luimneach a bhí,
Baile Átha Cliath atá,
Corcaigh a bheidh.
Limerick that was,
Dublin that is,
Cork that will be.

Spéir gan réiltín,
Tinteán gan leanbh.
A sky without a star,
A hearth without a child.

Bád gan stiúir nó cú gan eireaball.
Without a rudder a boat can't sail
And the hound can't run without its tail.

Ansiúd a bádh a choileáin.
'Twas there his pups drowned. [53]

Is é an scéal é á insint don chapall
is an capall ina chodladh.
Telling a story
To a horse that's snoring.[54]

Is leithide bualtrach satailt air.
Cowdung spreads when you walk on it.[55]

Mairg gur beag leis Dia mar lón.
Woe to him for whom God is little sustenance.

Ní hí an bhreáthacht a chuireann
an corcán ag fiuchadh.
Beauty won't boil the pot.

Seachain is ná taobhaigh,
Is ná tabhair an t-aitheantas ar aon rud.
Be on your guard and don't take sides
And on your life never sacrifice friends.

Fearr seanfhiacha na seanfhala.
Better old debts than old grudges.

Conas a bheadh an t-ubhaillín
Ach mar a bheadh an t-abhaillín?
Could the apple be
But as the apple tree?[56]

Gach éan mar a oiltear
Agus an naosc san abar.
Every bird as it is brought up
And the snipe in the mud.

Tart madra lá báistí.
The dog's thirst on a rainy day.[57]

34

An té nach bhfuil tobac aige cacadh sé ina phíp,
Arsa an fear nach raibh aon easpa air féin.
He who has no tobacco may he shit in his pipe,
Said the grouch with his pouch full.

Lá breá ag do chairde – dod adhlacan!
May your friends have a fine day – at your burial!

Go ndeine an diabhal dréimire
de chnámh do dhroma
Ag piocadh úll i ngairdín Ifrinn.
May the devil make a ladder of your backbone
And pluck apples in the garden of hell!

Nar gheala do chac ort!
May your shit never lighten![58]

Nílim im scoláire is ní háil liom a bheith ...
I'm not a scholar and have no wish to be ... [59]

Gach Ultach ar an ngunna;
Gach Connachtach ar an bpíce;
Gach Laighneach ar an gcapall
– Is iad rogha na bhfear na Muimhnigh.
Every Ulsterman to his gun;
Every Connaughtman to his pike;
Every Leinsterman to his horse
– It's the Munsterman I like.

Cad é an bac le mála na scadán
Boladh na scadán a bheith air?
What's wrong with a bag full of herring
That smells of herring?

Ariú nach é an fear é an bairneach – mar a dúirt
  an madarua.
Isn't the limpet some man, as the fox said.[60]

Cuir an sagart i lar an pharóiste.
Put the priest in the middle of the parish.[61]

Gealt a chuir tús leis an rince.
A loon invented dancing.[62]

Seacht scadán díol bradáin,
Seacht mbradán díol róin,
Seacht róin díol muice mara,
Seacht muca mara díol míl mhóir,
Seacht míol mhóra díol an cheannruáin chróin,
Seacht gceannruáin chrón díol an domhain mhóir.
Seven herrings: a meal for a salmon,
Seven salmon: a meal for a seal,
Seven seals: a meal for a porpoise,
Seven porpoises: a meal for a whale,
Seven whales: a meal for a smooth blenny,
Seven smooth blennies: a meal for the whole world.

Éisteacht na muice bradaí
D'aireodh sí an féar ag fás.
The thieving pig has ears on its ass
And she can hear the growing grass.

Lia gach boicht bás.
Death is every poor man's physician.

Maireann croí éadrom i bhfad.
The heart that's light lives long.

Is teoide don bhrat a dhúbladh.
The blanket's warmer when doubled.

Má thugann tú iasacht do chuid brístí
Ná gearr na cnaipí díobh.
If you're going to lend your trousers
Don't rip off the buttons.

Is doiligh stocaí a bhaint d'fhear coslomnocht.
It's hard to take the stockings off a barefoot man.

Is minic táilliúir agus drochthreabhsar air;
Is minic gréasaí agus drochbhróga faoi.
Many's the tailor with a bad pair of trousers;
Many's the cobbler with a bad pair of shoes.

Is mór orlach de shrón duine.
An inch is a lot on a nose.[63]

*Rud ar bith leis an ocras a mhaolú, arsa an táilliúir
    agus é ag ithe míoltóige.*
Anything to assuage the hunger, said the tailor swallow-
    ing a midge.[64]

*An rud nach leigheasann im nó uisce beatha,
níl leigheas air.*
If whiskey or butter don't work the cure
Then nothing at all will – and that's for sure.

*Is measa scríob sa lorga
ná buille den tua sa cheathrú.*
A scratch to the shin is worse than an axe to the
    thigh.

Is garbh mí na gcuach.
A month of squalls
When the cuckoo calls.

Chomh díomhaoin le ladhraicín píobaire.
As idle as a piper's little finger.

*Níl insan saol seo ach tréimhse mí-ámharach
Agus níl fhios ag éinne ó inniu go dtí amárach.*
This life is only a period of sorrow
And nobody knows from today to tomorrow.

Rud is mó 'thit amach ariamh
Ní raibh ann ach scéal naoi lá,
Mar do thiocfadh scéal eile ina dhiaidh
Do bhainfeadh an mheabhair as.
The greatest thing that ever occurred
Was only a nine-day wonder,
Then another story stirred
And tore it all asunder!

An té a luíonn le gadharaibh
éireoidh le dearnaitibh!
He who lies down with dogs at his ease
At morning will jump up – hopping with fleas!

Is fearr banlámh den lá
ná dhá bhanlámh den óiche.
A cubit of day is worth two cubits of night.[65]

An rud nach binn le duine ní chluineann sé é.
What's not sweet to the ear
We simply don't hear.

Níor bhlais an bia nach mblaisfidh an bás.
He who eats will be eaten![66]

Cuir an breac san eangach
sula gcuire tú sa phota é.
Net the fish
Before you serve the dish.[67]

Is minic a mhaolaigh béile maith brón.
Sorrows are never as real
After a good meal.

Cia mholfadh an ghé bhréan
Mura molfadh sí í féin?
The goose that looks like she has waded in swill,
If she won't praise herself – who else will?

Ní cluintear in Ifreann ach fead mná
agus blao circe.
Nothing is heard in the depths of hell
But a woman whistling and the cackle of a hen.

Go dtí La San Dic,
An lá nach dtig.
Until St Dick's day
Which won't come your way.

Cé phósfas an t-airgead, pósfaidh sé óinseach,
Imeoidh an t-airgead, fanfaidh an óinseach.
Marry the money, and marry the twit:
The money will go – but not the dim-wit.

Spur ar an gcois agus gan an chos ann
Is gan d'anam sa chorp ach ar nós cúr na habhann.
The spur on the heel – but the heel was a dream
And the soul in your body is but foam on a stream.

Murach m'athair
Dhéanfainn cathair.
Were it not for my father – more is the pity!
I'd be well on my way to building a city.

Smachtódh gach éinne drochbhean, ach an té a
    mbeadh sí aige.
An unruly woman is easy to control
Except when she happens to be your own.[68]

Ná díol caora dhubh;
Ná ceannaigh caora dhubh;
Ná bí gan caora dhubh.
Don't sell a black sheep;
Don't buy a black sheep;
Don't be without a black sheep.

Níl coill ar bith gan brosna a loiscithe.
Any forest can be fired by its own kindling [69]

Druid le fear na bruíne
agus gheobhaidh tú síocháin..
Face up to the trouble-maker and he'll leave you
    alone.

Cuairt an lao ar an athbhuaile.
The calf's visit to the disused milking-place.[70]

An ní nach bhfeiceann súil ní bhrónann croí.
The heart does not grieve what the eye cannot
  perceive.

Ní dhéanfadh an saol capall rása d'asal.
Whatever else might come to pass
You won't make a racehorse of an ass.

Is minic a bhíos fréamh cham ag crann díreach.
Many is the upright tree
With a branch as crooked as can be.

Níl sprid ná púca ar bith
Gan fios a chúise 'ge.
There's not a spirit or a pooka in the air
That doesn't know why he is there.

Na tabhair dod dhailtín cóir nach cuibhe dhó;
Ná comhluadar le huaislibh tíre;
Mura gcoinnír smachtaithe é is é 'choimeád foríseal
Is measa le cothú é ná coileán mac tíre.
Keep him away from the company of gentry;
Give him only what befits a child,
If you don't keep him strict within the bounds of
  decency
He'll be harder to rear than the wolves of the wild.

Bhéarfadh súgán cátha chun dlí thú
Is ní thabharfadh slabhra iarainn thar n-ais thú!
For a wisp of a straw
To the court of law
And an iron chain
Couldn't drag you back again!

Slaghdán Dhónaill
Slaghdán i gcónaí.
Donald has a cold –
He has that of old.

Ba chuma Donncha um Nollaig nó thall faoi Cháisc
Mar bhí Nollaig ag Donncha oíche is lá.
Dennis at Christmas or Dennis at Easter;
One and the same – Dennis always a-feasting.

Níor chodail an dris chosáin riamh.
All day, all night until dawn peeps,
The wayside bramble never sleeps.[71]

Ochón ó! An t-éan a bhí ar an gcrann,
Nuair a d'imigh sé ní raibh sé ann.
The bird on the tree, alas and alack!
Once he flew off he never came back!

Ceann dubh ar gach maidin earraigh
Agus eireaball seannaigh as san siar.
Spring morning: head all black,
Tail of a fox after that.

Ní thig meirg ar an eochair a mbaintear leas aisti.
The key that's used does not rust.

Seachain fearg ó fhear na foidhne.
Beware the anger of the patient man.

Gach re mbliain 'bhíonn an fia fireann.
Every second year the deer is a male.[72]

Fiach dubh fómhair nó fionnóg earraigh,
Droch-chomhartha iad do bheith ag screadaigh.
Autumn cormorant, scald-crow in spring
For them to be screeching – an unlucky thing.

Fuath dem fhuathaibh is cóir sin:
Ridire gan scian aige ar cóisir,
Fear liath d'iarraidh mná óige,
Buachailleacht cois luaithe an tráthnóna.
All the hates that are easiest to understand:
A knight without a knife at feasting time,
A grey-haired man seeking a young girl's hand,
At watch over ashes at evening time.

Is minic a bhí droch-chrú faoi chapall gabhann.
Many is the blacksmith's horse badly shod.

Is minic a chealg briathra míne cailín críonna.
Many a girl lost what can't be bought with money
And all because of words, sprinkled with honey.

46

Ceann cíortha a dhíolas na cosa.
Comb your hair and you're half-way there.[73]

Is fuar an rud clú gan chara.
Fame and glory – how terribly cold
If there's no hand to hold.

An té a chailleas a chlú cailleann a náire.
Lose your good name and you'll lose all shame.

Is minic a bhí cú mall sona.
Many a lagging dog came home – to find a bone.

Moill ar tí an deabhaidh.
As fast as you can go
It will only make you slow.[74]

Is mairg a mbeadh doicheall roimh dheacair aige.
If with difficulties he should meet –
Woe to him who sounds the retreat.

Ding de féin a scoilteas an leamhán.
A wedge of its own timber splits the elm.[75]

Ná déan acht agus ná bris acht.
Don't make a decree, don't break a decree.[76]

*An té a mbíonn an t-ádh ar maidin air bíonn sé air
    maidin agus tráthnóna.*
If you're in luck at the break of day
All day long your luck will stay.[77]

Ná baintear an t-ainm den bhlonag.
If it's fat – call it that!

48

Is maith an t-anlann an t-ocras.
If it's hunger you feel –
That's sauce on your meal.

Is fearr bail ná iomad.
Enough is better than too much.

*Níor tháinig riamh an mheidhir mhór nach
    dtiocfadh ina diaidh an dobrón.*
There never was pure joy without alloy.

Is díon an crann fad is díon dó féin é.
A tree will give you shelter as long as it shelters
    itself.[78]

Briseann an dúchas trí chrúba an chait.
Nature, following its own laws,
Breaking out in the cat's paws.

Folaíonn grá gráin.
Love veils the unlovely.

Is geal leis an bhfiach dubh a ghearrcach féin.
The raven thinks its nestling
Is a bright thing!

Is fearr bothán lán ná caisleán mór folamh.
Better the hovel of plenty
Than the castle that's empty.

Is leor don dreoilín a nead.
The nest of the wren is as much as it needs.

Buíochas do Dhia is do Mhuire,
Ach mura bhfuair mé go leor
Fuair mé oiread is duine eile.
Thanks be to God and His holy mother,
If I didn't get a lot, I got as much as the other!

Más crúsca thú seachain an corcán.
A jug should not consort with a pot.

Ná bíodh aon chat ach cat a mharós luch.
Let's have no cat in the house
That will not catch a mouse.

Ag cur claí timpeall goirt leis an gcuach a
    choinneáill istigh.
Fencing the field to keep in the cuckoo.

Is maol gualainn gan bhráthair.
A shoulder is bare
Without a brother's hand to care.

Ní heolas go haontíos, ní haontíos go pluid,
ní pluid go bliain.
To know me? Live with me my dear
And share my blanket, at least for a year.

Is uaigneach an níochán nach mbíonn léine ann!
That laundry is sad – not a shirt to be had!

Is fearr rith maith ná drochsheasamh.
Better to run while you can
Than stand like a man.

*Tabhair an mhóin abhaile agus cuirfidh mé tine
    mhór síos.*
You fetch the turf and I'll light the fire.

*Dhá ní gan náire, tart is grá, ach thug an tochas
    an barr leis.*
No shame being thirsty, or making love –
But scratching? Heavens above!

Ní bheathaíonn na briathra na bráithre.
Fables won't fatten the friars.

*Grá don chomhluadar a thugas na gadhair chuig
    an Aifreann.*
With an hour or two to pass
The dogs come to Mass.

*An coileach ag déanamh cothrom na Féinne i measc
    na gcearc.*
The cockerel cherishing his hens equally.

Níl tuile dá mhéad nach dtránn.
No matter how great
The flood will abate.

Is fearr an t-imreas ná an t-uaigneas.
Rather strife
Than a lonely life.

An t-aonú aithne dhéag – tabhair aire duit féin.
The eleventh commandment – look after yourself.

Níor loisc seanchat é féin riamh.
An old cat never scorched himself.

Síoda buí ar Shiobhán agus gioblachaí ar a hathair.
There's Siobhán in her silks of gold
And there is her father, raggedy and cold.

*Is éasca dhá shimléar a dhéanamh ná tine a
    choinneáil i gceann acu.*
Easier to build two chimneys than keep a fire going
    in one of them.

Trí rud nach raibh riamh ann:
Nead ag luich i gcluais cait,
Giorria i seid con,
Gé ar gor i bpluais madarua.
Three things that never have been:
A mouse's nest in a cat's ear,
A hare in the hound's kennel,
A hatching goose in a fox's den.

Trí shaghas inchinne:
Inchinn reatha,
Inchinn chloiche,
Inchinn chéarach.
Three types of mind:
The volatile mind,
The mind of stone,
The mind of wax.[79]

Trí trioblóidí mhná na Rinne:
Páistí,
Prátaí,
Is truscar!
The women of Ring are troubled indeed:
Children,
Potatoes,
Cast-up sea-weed![80]

Trí nithe chuaigh de Harry Stottle a thuiscint:
Intinn na mban,
Obair na mbeach,
Agus teacht is imeacht na taoide.
Aristotle was stumped by these:
The mind of a woman,
The ebb and flow of the tide,
The work of the bees.

Súil, glúin, uille – na trí rud is leochailí.
The easiest to hurt are these three:
The eye,
The elbow,
And the knee.

Dá mba ór an duille donn thíolacfadh Fionn é.
If the autumn leaves were gold, Fionn would give
   it away.[81]

Doras feasa fiafraí.
Questioning is the door to knowledge.

Ní ghabhann dorn dúnta seabhac.
A closed hand doesn't catch a hawk.

Turas na gcearc go Críoch Lochlann.
It's the hens' journey to Scandinavia.[82]

Ní i gcónaí a mharaíonn Daidín fia.
Daddy doesn't always kill a deer.[83]

An luibh ná fachtar a fhóineann.
The herb that cures is the one that can't be found.

Ní dhíolann dearmad fiacha.
Forgetting does not repay a debt.

Uaisle éisteas le healaín.
It's a sign of nobility to patronise the arts.[84]

Trí nithe is sia ina bhfanann a rian:
Rian guail i gcoill,
Rian siséil i líg,
Agus rian soic i gcrích.
Three things which leave the longest-lasting traces:
Trace of charcoal on wood,
Trace of chisel on stone,
Trace of ploughshare on furrow.

Beagán ar bheagán
Mar a itheann an cat an scadán.
Little by little –
As the cat eats the herring.

Fear gan bean mar asal gan eireaball.
A man without a woman, like
a donkey without a tail

Is olc an bhean bheo ná cuirfeadh bean mharbh.
It's a bad living woman who can't bury a dead one.
(i.e. a woman who can't bury the memory of a
   deceased first wife).

Is fearr a bheith i do pheata ag seanfhear ná i do
   sclábhaí ag fear óg.
Better be an old man's pet than a young man's
   slave.

Giorraíonn beirt bóthar.
Two shorten a road.

Dá mbeadh spré ag an gcat is minic a pógfaí a béal.
If he cat had a dowry, it's often her mouth would
   be kissed.

Trí búada téiti:
Ben cháemh
Ech maith
Cú luath.
Three glories of a gathering:
Fine wife
Good steed
Speedy hound.

Trí athghin an domhain:
Brú mná
Úth bó
Neas gabhann.
Three renewals of the world
Woman's womb
Cow's udder
Smith's fiery furnace.

Is treise toil ná tuiscint.
Will is stronger than understanding.

Tá Dia láidir agus máthair mhaith aige.
God is strong and he has a good mother.

Níl in uasal agus íseal
Ach thuas seal agus thíos seal.
The lowly and the high
Are only up and down a while.

Adharc bó, crúb capaill,
drannadh madra, agus gáire Shasanaigh.
A cow's horn, a horse's hoof,
a dog's snarl, an Englishman's laugh.

Ní hionann bhur nDia Connachtach
Agus Dia breá fairsing na nUltach.
Your Connacht God is not the same
As the generous Ulster God, praise be his name.

Nuair a imíonn an séan, faigheann an fhéile gás.
When happiness goes, generosity dies.

Gach duine ar a shon féin, agus Dia ar son an uile!
Everyone for himself, and God for us all!

Ná caith do chuid i d'aonar.
Do not eat alone.

Is beag an deoir fola nach teo í ná uisce.
Few are the drops of blood not warmer than water.

Deartháir don bhréag an béal bán.
Flattery is a brother of the lie.

Sáraíonn eagna gach saibhreas.
Wisdom surpasses all wealth.

Is trom an t-ualach an leisce.
Laziness is a heavy load.

59

Sagart balbh, sagart dealbh.
Dumb priest, poor priest.

Ná pós bean gan locht.
Don't marry a faultless woman.

Cá bhfuil sneachta na bliana anuraidh?
Where is last year's snow?

Trí ní a thagann gan iarraidh: grá, éad agus eagla.
Three things that come unasked: love, jealousy
  and fear.

Níl tuile nach dtránn ach tuile na ngrást.
All floods abate but the flood of grace.

*Char chaith fear ariamh carbhat muinéil chomh
  deas le lámha a pháiste féin.*
No man never wore a neck-tie as nice as the hands
  of his own child.

A bhuí le Dia nach é saor an bháid a dhein an tigh!
Thank God it wasn't the boatwright built the
  house! (said on a very wet day)

*Ní fios cé is túisce craiceann na seanchaorach nó
  na caorach óige ar an bhfraith.*
One can't say whether the skin of the old sheep
  or that of the young sheep will be the first to
  hang from the rafter.

Ná gearradh do theanga do scornach.
Let your tongue not cut your throat.

Beirbh birín dom is beireod birín duit.
Cook a *birín* for me and I'll cook one for you.[85]

Ní cuimhnítear ar an arán a itear.
Eaten bread is not remembered.

Deacair giorria a chur as tor nach mbeidh sé.
Difficult to drive a hare out of a bush if he's not
    in it.

Ní baintear fuil as tornapa.
Blood is not drawn from a turnip.

Fearr le himirt féin ná mac le hól.
Better a son given to gambling than to drink.

Súil le cúiteamh a lomann an cearrbhach.
The next 'good thing' ruins the gambler.

Beag sochar na síormheisce.
Little profit in being constantly pissed!

Bean ar meisce, pis in aisce.
Drunken woman, free ride.[86]

Maith an mustard an sliabh.
The mountain is a good mustard.[87]

Is luachmhar an t-anam, mar a dúirt an táilliúir agus é ag rith ón ngandal.

Life is precious, as the tailor said, fleeing from the gander.

Muca ciúine a itheann triosc.
Still swine guzzle hogwash.

Sroichfidh each mall muilleann.
A slow horse will reach the mill.

Cad a dhéanfadh mac an chait ach luch a mharú.
What would the cat's son do but kill a mouse.

Déanann codladh fada tóin leis an duine.
Sleep long and you'll have no arse to your trousers.[88]

Bíonn cosa crua ar chapall iasachta.
A borrowed horse is hard of foot.[89]

Is beag an dealg a dhéanfadh braon.
The tiniest thorn can suppurate.

Níor dhún Dia doras riamh nár oscail sé ceann eile.
God never closes one door without opening
    another.

An bhean atá dóighiúil is furasta a cóiriú.
A handsome woman is easily dressed.

Éist mórán agus can beagán.
Hear much, say little.
Is taibhseach iad adharca na mbó thar lear.
Foreign cows have long horns.[90]

Meileann muilte Dé go mall.
God's mill grinds slow.

Is olc an t-éan a shalaíonn a nead féin.
It's a bad bird that fouls its own nest.

Ní hé lá na gaoithe lá na scolb.
The windy day is no day for scollops.[91]

Is olc an chearc nach scríobann di féin.
It's a poor hen that won't scratch for herself.

Tosach sláinte codladh.
Sleep is the first sign of recovery.

Tuar an t-ádh agus tiocfaidh sé!
Predict good fortune and it will come!

Ag caitheamh an tsaoil is an saol ár gcaitheamh.
We consume time while she consumes us.

Paidir chapaill
A horse's prayer.[92]

Is mairg a d'imreadh a mháthair orthu.
Woe to him who'd bet his mother on them!

Is fuirist gabháil thar dhoras duine mhairbh
Nuair ná bionn sé féin ná a mhadra istigh.
It is easy to pass the dead man's door
When himself and his dog aren't there anymore.

Na trí ní is mó giodam:
Piscín cait,
Meannán gabhair,
Nó baintreach óg mhná.
The three friskiest things:
The kitten,
The kid goat,
The young widow.

Bainne as diaidh feola agus uisce as diaidh éisc.
Milk after meat and water after fish.[93]

D'íosfadh sé an gharbhach.
He'd eat the robin-run-the-hedge.[94]

Is trom an t-ualach putóga folmha.
Empty intestines are a heavy load.

Bia rí ruacain,
Bia buachalla bairnigh,
Bia caillí miongáin,
Is í á bpiocadh le snáthaid.
Cockles food for a king,
Limpets food for a youth,
Food for old hags periwinkles,
And they picking them with a pin.

A bhuachaill, beir buartha go bpósfair
Is an uair sin beir buartha do dhóthain!
Boy, you'll be troubled till you're married –
And then you'll be properly harried![95]

Cion gan fhios do mhnaoi nó leanbh.
Love unbeknown to woman or child.[96]

An chéad ghrá mná agus an dara grá fir.
A woman's first love, a man's second love.[97]

Bod seanduine nó cíoch seanmhná.
An old man's penis, an old woman's breast.[98]

Is minic a bheir dall ar ghiorria.
Many's the blind man caught a hare.[99]

Ná feic a bhfeicir;
Is ná clois a gcloisir;
Is má fiafraítear díot
Abair ná feadrais.
Hear not what you hear;
See not what you see;
And if you're asked
Say 'Don't ask me!'

Cosa gloine fúibh is go mbrise siad!
Glass legs under you – and may they break![100]

Dioc ort!
Pip on you![101]

Nár mhúcha Dia solas na bhflaitheas orainn!
May God not quench the light of heaven on us![102]

NOTES

1   Meanness.

2   Might be said of you when you're completely unconcerned with proceedings.

3   A superstition, to be ignored at your peril.

4   Say goodbye to something lost forever.

5   This one can be used to spare somebody a trip to India to see his guru again.

6   How to cut a fish.

7   The reference to entrails should be understood in the context of Ireland's gory history.

8   Say this of a small nasty person.

9   A cure for what ails you.

10   Just in case you're worried, all these omens are supposed to occur more or less at the same time.

11   A spouse or flat-mate might utter this at your miserable attempts at making a fire.

12   Children hear more than we realise.

13 One could use this when your partner for dinner wonders what may be edible or merely decorative.

14 It's hard to work on an empty stomach.

15 Every community has its own oddball, or genius.

16 The Irish actually says the three fastest *fish*. The seal is not a fish but takes its place in the triad by dint of alliteration.

17 The overwhelming popularity of the triad form in Irish proverbiology greatly facilitated my introduction of the *haiku* form to Irish prosody. The triad is one of the oldest forms of native oral literature and to this day you can still hear dozens of them from the older generation of native speakers.

18 Forever.

19 The slow messenger who never returns.

20 Children used to say this to the last straggling crow, which often had the effect of the crow getting into another gear and maybe even heading the posse!

21 Not quite as piggish as it sounds: natural metaphors for stubborness, flightiness and docility.

22 Not necessarily a black sheep, mind you!

23 Applicable to 'dedicated followers of fashion'.

24 Unnecessary parsimoniousness. It is said that the moorhen only eats what's between her feet.

25 A warning not to be ostentatious.

26 The lot – the whole shooting gallery.

27 Something prized, though not deservedly so.

28 The poor selfless creature is left with slim pickings.

29 A time no one remembers.

30 When he couldn't get his paws on them he declared they were sour.

31 A reference to the mouse's prodigious sex-life and, by imputation, to any Casanova – or maenad.

32 It was believed that if you slept outside, the newt would invade you and gobble up your food as fast as you were swallowing it.

33 One eye open! The hare looms large in oral Irish literature. A saying I was much taken by, when I first visited the Dingle peninsula, was *chomh scaipthe le mún giorria* – as scattered as a hare's piss. The animal, seemingly, urinates on the run.

34 He had a great feast but was left with no sheep.

35 Superfluous additions! The pig is an important character in oral and written literature. It occurs plentifully in place-names, such as Ros Muc, the peninsula of pigs. The Irish are inordinately fond of bacon. The sacred druidic tree of pre-Christian times was the oak. Pigs ate of the fruit of the oak – acorns – and, by symbiosis, were themselves sacred.

36 Someone who might turn on you after your having done him a good deed.

37 When it's best not to cut corners.

38   He's caught a Tartar! Reminds me a bit of the
      definition of a university professor – the un-
      sackable teaching the unteachable, or the
      huntsman – the unspeakable in pursuit of the
      uneatable! Word-play in Irish, however, rarely
      relies on punning, Spoonerisms and the like.
      The notorious 'Irish bull' – a ludicrous blunder
      – may have come from language-shift, from
      Irish to English, as when the returned Yank,
      distressed to see the pig in the kitchen, ex-
      claimed: 'Extinguish that pig at once!'

39   Easier to blacken someone's reputation than to
      restore it.

40   Various eminences, Aristotle, Dean Swift,
      Cromwell, Julia of Norwich, Henry the Eighth,
      Napoleon, as well as a host of Irish poets, most
      notably Eoghan Rua Ó Súilleabháin, have found
      their way, for different reasons, to the Gaelic
      Pantheon of Immortals.

41   A rainy day, bad for turf, good for cabbage.

42   Humility in the great.

43   Dealing with people.

44   The cow has been so dominant in Ireland that
      she is Ireland herself – 'silk of the kine', *Droim-
      eann Donn Dílis*. Our sacred river, the Boyne/
      Bóinn means 'fair cow' and is linguistically
      cognate with the Sanscrit, *Govinda*, another
      name for *Krishna*. However, the Indo-European
      question is a minefield. We do not have a
      modern etymological dictionary in Irish to tell
      us that the word for a road, *bóthar*, is related

to *bó*, a cow – the width to allow one cow to pass another.

45   The pooka was a dominant elemental in Irish life. One researcher, Deasún Breatnach, is of the opinion that the word may be related to the Greek *psyche*, in which the *y* is sounded much like a *u*. The Liffey has its origins in *Poll an Phúca* (the Pooka's Hole). The *púca na sméar* for instance, or berry-pooka, was responsible for the blight on berries in the autumn. The pooka is as large as life in Flann O'Brien's classic novel, *At Swim-Two-Birds.*

46   Ireland has one of the most important gannet colonies in Europe, situatedon the enchanting Skelligs.

47   I must say I've never heard this one. In Dunquin, County Kerry, the lovely comparison used was that of the 'caobach', a sea-bird known to stand on one leg on a rock some distance from the shore! Thus, 'bhí caobach air' – he was mad drunk.

   Staying with ornithological imagery I once saw five pints of stout perched on a counter and a local wit observed: *Féach na fiaigh mhara* – 'would you look at the cormorants!'

48   Said of those too fond of idle pleasures and aping the gentry.

49   John used to bring the ram to Cahirciveen, not to sell – as you might think – but as an excuse to go on a batter. The ram got so accustomed

to this pilgrimage that he'd make his own way home.

50 Said of something that's just right – say, an appropriate gift.

51 Fog.

52 The traditionally preferred way to go.

53 Said of someone in his habitual haunt, such as the local pub: the mother of pups frequently visits the spot where they were drowned. Liam O'Flaherty's story, *Bás na Bó*, is an eloquent testimony to maternal instincts in animals. The proverb suggests that paternal instincts also exist!

54 Said of a disinterested listener.

55 Some things are best left unsaid.

56 Well, in these days of genetic engineering – who knows?

57 When someone asks for a drink and it's not the thirst that's killing him.

58 Black heavy faeces are a sign of ill-health.

59 That's what the fox is supposed to have said to the donkey, admitting that he didn't know what was written on the horse's hoof. The donkey was sure that he could decipher it and asked the horse to show him the hoof. Well, he got the hoof all right – and that was the end of him.

60 The limpet was on a rock, as is his wont, one sunny day. Along came the fox and thought he'd enjoy a little delicacy. He slipped his tongue under the half-open shell. The limpet

closed tightly. The tide came in and drowned the fox.

61 The 'priest' concerned here is a basket of boiled potatoes set in the middle of the floor for all to share. By the way, *sagairtín* can mean a little priest or an inedible periwinkle! Irish is notorious for the variety of applications of words which look and sound alike. Thus, *gealach* is the word for moon, or a thin slice of turnip. Dineen's Dictionary is a treasure-trove of such multiple meanings, layered upon one another. For instance *donn* is the colour brown, also the heart of a tree, also a prince, also 'the name of a fairy inhabiting sandbanks off the Clare coast'!

62 *Rince* is from the English 'ring', as in ring-dances. Curiously, there is no native Irish word for dancing.

63 Suitable as a motto on the wall in a plastic surgeon's waiting-room.

64 The tailor is a very popular figure in Irish folklore, almost as popular as the legendary Góbán Saor, the Master stonemason. In our own time the most famous tailor was from Gúgán Barra and is immortalised in *The Tailor and Ansty* by Eric Cross (Mercier Press). Once an eminent Cork sculptor came to do the Tailor's head. A neighbour called and declared that it was most unnatural for any man to have two heads! [The Tailor was a fine speaker, un-tainted by Victorian attitudes to bodily func-

tions and his outpourings got him into trouble with the puritan clergy and the cleric-ridden state censorship of the time.]

65 A warning against working late at night. The *banlámh* was an old Irish cloth measurement of 21 inches – in West Kerry 24 inches.

66 Death.

67 Or, as good old Mrs Beaton used to say in relation to hare soup – first catch your hare.

68 Had there been more women employed gathering lore for the Folklore Commission we might have a more balanced war between the sexes.

69 Every Achilles has a heel.

70 Nostalgic visit home.

71 Sources of annoyance on your path.

72 Offspring.

73 Good grooming compensates for many defects.

74 *Festina lente.*

75 Diamond cut diamond.

76 Follow traditional ways.

77 Begin well – end well.

78 Until it becomes saturated.

79 Wax here denotes 'retentive'.

80 Ring is a beautiful seaside area in County Waterford where some Irish is still spoken, in a very distinctive dialect. It produced such luminaries as poet Áine Ní Fhoghlú, singer Nioclás Tóibín and Seán Ó Cuirrín who translated *Dracula* into mellifluous Irish.

81 Fionn MacCumhaill, the mythical Celtic figure

who gave his name to Wien/Vienna.

82   No chance of going back again. It was believed that the Vikings brought hens to Ireland.

83   Cause for a minor celebration.

84   Said by some poor poet or other... well, he would, wouldn't he!

85   Birín is a diminutive of bior rósta, a roasting spit.

86   *Pis* is the Irish for vagina and also, because of a resemblance, a pea-pod.

87   Appetiser.

88   *Leis*, in Irish, can mean: 'also', 'a thigh', 'of his' and 'naked' so that '*bhí leis leis leis leis*' translates as 'a thigh of his was also bare'.

89   Borrowing can lead to abuse.

90   Distance lends enchantment to a view.

91   The scollop is a looped stick for securing thatch on a roof.

92   Endless rigmarole. The ploughing horse that stumbled on his knees spent a long time thus – as if in prayer.

93   The traditionally preferred drink with meat and fish respectively. When the potato took over in pre-Famine Ireland much lore about food and hundreds of recipes were lost to later generations. Does anybody know today how the vegetable dish, *sancam soncam*, was prepared? Has anybody today tasted bread made from acorn flour? Were shamrocks used as a salad ingredient? Why did well-known lunatics, such as Suibhne Geilt (Mad Sweeney), have a

preference for watercress? Those early Gaelic Leaguers who hoped for a revival of the ancestral language, traditional music, dress and so on, seem to have overlooked food.

94 He'd eat anything at all. Robin-run-the-hedge is also known as cleavers or clivers, or goose-grass. Very prickly.

95 At least the Brehon Laws allowed for divorce and listed among unnatural cruelties – giving grounds for divorce – excessive wind in one's partner's intestines.

96 If women or children know that they are loved they will take advantage of it.

97 These are the most enduring.

98 Drooping – God save the mark! Given the natural curiosity that children have about sex it's amazing how few children know the Irish for 'penis' – a reflection on the unnatural sterilised manner in which the language has been taught in schools. Words for 'penis' include: *toilfhéith, slat, bod, crann, pilbín, an fear bán, an ball fearga* and a boy's penis is *sceidín*!

99 A sarcastic proverb when you don't believe a word of someone's boasting.

100 Said to hens!

101 Pip is a disease in poultry, hawks etc. Thus the expression 'he gives me the pip!'

102 Said on putting out the light.